1

Routines, Rhythms, & Schedules

How to Simplify Life With Kids

By Rachel Normal and Lauren Tamm

Plus 20+ Free Printables to Get You Started!

For our kids who make each day a unique parenting adventure.

For our husbands who support us each and every day.

For all the moms who are looking to simplify life with kids. You are among friends!

Contents

Foreword

I love routine! What can I say? I was a teacher, and now I am a mom to four young children. Routine isn't just helpful for me, but it is helpful for our kids. It lets them know what is going to come next, what they can expect and what our day will look like. Routines help to eliminate temper tantrums, mood swings, and chaos, in most cases.

I find that by embracing a rhythm and routine with our kids, our days flow more smoothly. I walk them through our routine at the beginning of each day. They know that after breakfast, they get dressed for school and make their beds. It isn't anything that we need to go back and forth on, because it is simply part of their routine. Our routines offer them a sense of security because they know what comes next and they feel confident in it. Plus, it gives us time to connect, because as part of our routine, we snuggle at night while we read books. They look forward to this, knowing it is a special part of the end of our day.

I love this book because it really showcases how beneficial rhythms, routines and schedules will be for your family and you will learn exactly what you need to do to make it work. I can't stress enough how great this will be to your family!

— Becky Mansfield, Your Modern Family

1

Introduction

I was shocked when I learned I was pregnant with my firstborn. I had plans that didn't yet include a baby, and much to my surprise, I found myself preparing to be a stay-at-home mom. We were in the middle of moving countries (continents even!) so I had all the time in the world to do prenatal videos and read books. I read and read and read, and one of the most common threads found in various types of parenting books was this: find a routine that works for you and stick with it.

So that's exactly what I did. The first few months of my daughter's life were stressful for us adults, but we still managed to maintain a good routine. In fact, I found motherhood such an enjoyable experience that just one year later, I gave birth to a son. 15 months later, I gave birth to another son. And 16 months after that, I gave birth to a third son. Call me crazy (I know my family does), but the reason I'm able to parent four children four years of age and under is because we have good routines.

Our routines aren't set in stone and may change from month to month, but it's the number one thing I suggest to new mothers: get a good routine. It helps children sleep better, cope better with changes, and even behave better. Quite simply, it's the backbone of our days. If you are wondering what type of routine may work for you, this book is the place. We hope you find a routine that works well for your family and you reap the benefits daily.

—Rachel, A Mother Far from Home

During my first pregnancy, I did everything I could to prepare. From books and classes to seeking advice from other moms, I wanted to empower myself with as much knowledge as possible. Even so, in the first few months of my son's life, I found myself struggling far more than I imagined. I quickly discovered that taking care of a baby isn't as easy as it looks.

Something changed as soon as my son turned 6 weeks old though—we found our rhythm, we developed a good schedule, and we never looked back. Two years later as my husband and I prepare for the birth of our second child, it's hard to imagine our life without rhythms, routines, and schedules. It simplifies our life, facilitates easier parenting, and makes for less stressful days.

Some may argue that regular routines and schedules stifle your life. That it's not realistic to live daily life by an approximate schedule without feeling too restricted or confined. Personally, I find the exact opposite to be true. The schedule brings freedom. Because the schedule offers predictability in our lives, it's easy to find times during the day that are perfect for outings, errands, and of course, sleep.

Schedules, routines, and rhythms are so empowering to our family that I'm passionate about sharing our success in order to help others. It is my hope that through this book, you will find a rhythm that works well for your family, simplifies your life, and brings

more freedom and predictability to your parenting
journey than you ever imagined.

—Lauren, The Military Wife and Mom

2

Getting Started With a Good Schedule

The benefits of a routine are undeniable. You know what to expect. The kids know what to expect, and daily life runs smoother. Whether you are more structured or embrace unscheduled time, you can still enjoy a daily routine or rhythm that can transform your home from one of chaos to one of calm.

What's a Routine?

Routine can mean:
- Regularity and consistency within your day
- A series of "one thing happens before another" actions

- Using the clock as a guide (whether general or specific) for the day's activities

Routine need not mean:
- Letting the clock be your master
- Always doing the same things every day
- Throwing spontaneity out the window

The major events of the day make up the foundation of the routine. For little ones, this includes sleep, eating, and play. From infants to preschoolers, these still remain the most important activities. If you are creating a routine from scratch, start with times of your choosing for the basics, then add in all the extras.

Benefits of a Routine

The benefits of routine are widely documented and accepted. In fact, many successful business people and entrepreneurs will go so far as to say that eating the same exact thing every morning for breakfast is part of their routine. Why? They want to save all their decision-making bandwidth for more important daily tasks. While we don't need to be that rigid, this example serves as a reminder that a routine can allow us to save much of our energy for the important things.

Routines are beneficial for children because they:
- Give a sense of security and stability
- Help develop self-discipline
- Eliminate power battles
- Breed cooperation (children like to do what's next when they know what it is)
- Help the family find a good sleep rhythm

A Helpful Rhythm When Getting Started

One of the rhythms shared frequently throughout this book is the eat, wake, sleep rhythm.

What does the eat, wake, sleep rhythm mean exactly?

This simply means that when your child wakes from sleep, he or she will eat shortly thereafter. Then he will be awake for a bit and play. After that, he will rest again. The cycle repeats throughout the day as needed. The child does not always have a period of rest between each eat and play cycle, especially as he gets older and requires less daytime rest. This rhythm is common during infancy and the early toddler years, then it fades naturally over time as the child enters the school-aged years.

Why is this rhythm helpful?

Very young children—babies and toddlers—have the most energy to eat a good meal immediately after resting. Following the meal, kids can play and have fun and be silly. After a period of time, kids rest. The idea is to offer young kids the greatest opportunity to take a good full meal and fill their bellies when they have the most energy. This rhythm also helps young kids avoid eating and falling asleep mid-meal, only to wake up hungry a short period of time later. Overall, this rhythm helps encourage a more peaceful home with well-fed and well-rested kids.

Knowing Your Child's Sleep Needs

Learning and understanding how much sleep your child needs, based on averages for his age, can help immensely when creating a routine and rhythm. We created this chart to help you determine what your child may need. (Note: Sleep needs are based on averages.)

Average Sleep Needs By Age

Age	Total Sleep	Average Awake Time	Number of Naps
Birth - 6 weeks	16-18 hours	45-60 minutes	Varies
2-3 months	15-17 hours	1-1.5 hours	3-4+ naps
4-6 months	14-16 hours	1.5-2.5 hours	3-4 naps
7-9 months	14-15.5 hours	2.25-3 hours	2-3 naps
9-12 months	13-15 hours	2.75-4 hours	2 naps
12-18 months	12-14 hours	3-6 hours	1-2 naps
18-24 months	12-14 hours	4-6 hours	1 nap
2-3 years	12-14 hours	5-6 hours	1 nap
4-5 years	11-13 hours	12 hours	rest time no naps

For the Breastfeeding Mom

It's important to make note that if you are a breastfeeding mom with an young infant, you will want to have a well-established milk supply before starting a routine or schedule with your baby. After you pick up a nice rhythm and are ready for a schedule, the times are always approximate and intended to remain flexible. Always feed your baby on demand when needed, paying close attention to growth spurts and hunger cues. If your child is truly hungry, you never need to delay a feeding.

If you are uncomfortable with using the clock to set the flow for your day, pay close attention to the sample rhythms that are flexible depending upon your baby's own habits. See Chapters 13 and 14 for daily rhythms without set times and see Section 3 for printable daily rhythms.

Section One: Sample Schedules

3

6 Weeks to 3 Months Old

During the first 4 to 6 weeks of life, you do not need to stress yourself over a schedule. This period of time is all about finding little rhythms throughout the day and getting to know your baby. After several weeks pass and you start to settle into your new life, you may start a schedule when both you and your baby feel ready.

The following schedules in this chapter are common for babies anywhere from one to three months of age. **Always add more feedings if needed. Always feed your baby if he is hungry.** You simply do not need to put off a feeding in order to stick to an approximate schedule. For the first few months of your baby's life, you may often cluster fed every two hours in the evening. It's common for a baby to be very fussy during that time, and regardless if your baby is truly hungry or not, you may find nursing offers a great sense of comfort during that challenging part of the day.

Feel free to use these schedules as a guide and get creative making adjustments to suit the needs of your baby and your family.

Note: All schedules are approximate. Please use these as a guide for your day, but avoid feeling like the clock is your master.

Sample Schedule 1

- 7:00 am wake up for the day, eat, play
- 8:00 am nap
- 9:30 am wake, eat, play
- 10:30 am nap
- 12:00 pm wake, eat, play
- 1:00 pm nap
- 2:30 pm wake, eat, play
- 3:30 pm nap
- 5:00 pm wake, eat, play

- 6:30 pm bedtime routine, bath, eat
- 7:00 pm bedtime, down for the night
- 10:00-11:00 pm dreamfeed (if desired)
- 11:00 pm - 7:00 am night feeds (as many as your baby needs)

A Quick Note About the Dreamfeed

Because this is the first mention of the dreamfeed, we wanted to briefly share what a dreamfeed is and how to complete a dreamfeed if you so desire.

The dreamfeed is a feeding given to the baby right before mom and dad go to bed with the goal of preventing the baby from waking up just after you drift off to sleep. The feeding is typically offered about three hours after the baby is already in bed for the night.

The best time to offer a dreamfeed is approximately three hours after baby's bedtime meal. Assuming your baby goes to bed between 6:00 and 8:00 pm, the dreamfeed should be given somewhere between 10:00 pm and 11:00 pm. Any later and you will disturb night sleep. Any earlier and the baby won't really be hungry enough. Using only a night light, pick the baby up in the dark and offer the baby a feeding that is similar in ounces to a daytime feeding. Attempt to feed the baby as much as he will eat. After the feeding, offer a burp and then lay him back down.

The main purpose of the dreamfeed is to match up a baby's longer stretch of sleep with your longer stretch of sleep to help you feel more rested in the long run. The dreamfeed is 100 percent optional but is something to try if you think it will help.

Sample Schedule 2

If you are struggling with a baby who is a chronic 45-minute napper, this is a great schedule to work around your particular baby's sleep habits. Many babies struggle with short naps (some for weeks, others for months). This is what we refer to as a Sleep Cycle Transition Issue. What does that mean exactly? For a baby, sleep cycles last approximately 45 minutes; for adults, sleep cycles are about 90 minutes. If your baby struggles to nap longer than 45 minutes, it often means that he reached a period of light sleep in the cycle and for whatever reason could not remain asleep and transition into the next sleep cycle.

Chronic 45-minute naps can wreak havoc on your brain as a parent, often causing you to wonder why your baby won't sleep well. This can also make a schedule challenging when naps are erratic and unpredictable.

One thing you can do is use a sleep prop (such as a swing, bouncer, or sling) once per day to ensure one good long nap, then simply go with your baby's sleep flow the remainder of the day.

- 7:00 am wake, eat, play
- 8:00 am nap
- 8:45 am wake, eat, play
- 9:45 am nap
- 10:30 am wake, eat, play
- 11:30 am long nap in swing
- 2:30 pm wake, eat, play
- 4:00 pm nap
- 4:45 pm wake, eat, play
- 6:30 pm bedtime routine, bath, eat
- 7:00 pm bedtime, down for the night
- 10:00-11:00 pm dreamfeed (if desired)
- 11:00 pm - 7:00 am night feeds (as many as your baby needs)

Handwritten annotations in left margin: 6:30, 7:30, 8:15, 9:15, 10:00, 12:00, 12:30, 1:30, 2:15, 3:15-5:15 nap, 5:15-6:30 eat play, Bath eat, 7 Bedtime

25

Sample Schedule 3

You may prefer for your baby to be on a bit of a later schedule. Some parents really enjoy this if they have multiple children. Having the baby on a later schedule allows you to get the other kids going in the morning while the baby is still asleep. Likewise, it allows you to put the other children to bed while the baby is napping and frees you up to have quality alone time with the baby in the late evening before you head to bed yourself.

- 8:30 am wake, eat, play
- 9:30 am nap
- 11:30 am wake, eat, play
- 12:30 pm nap
- 2:30 pm wake, eat, play
- 3:30 pm nap
- 5:30 pm wake, eat, play
- 6:30 pm nap
- 8:00 pm wake, eat, play
- 9:00 pm bedtime routine, bath, eat
- 9:30 pm bedtime, down for the night
- 9:30 pm - 8:30 am night feeds (as many as your baby needs)

A Quick Note on Naps

Schedules and rhythms for young babies help lay the foundation for healthy sleep habits down the road, and routines help to make the world a more predictable place for a baby to enjoy. One thing you might wonder is how do I leave the house when the baby naps all the time?

The answer is simple: Do the best you can and leave the house when need be. In our home, I typically try to get in a few good naps for the baby and then run errands. You may find something different works particularly well for you. You can find balance by aiming to protect naps the majority of the time and doing what needs to be done the remainder.

4

3-6 Months Old

A 3-hour schedule is most common from 2-6 months. Some babies can tolerate a 3-hour schedule earlier than 2 months old. It really depends on how much your baby weighed at birth, how long your baby can stay awake, and how many feedings your baby requires during the daytime. I personally prefer to wait until at least 3 months before starting a 3-hour schedule.

Likewise, if you are feeding more frequently than every 3 hours during the night, you may want to stay on a 2.5-hour schedule for a bit longer until your baby drops a night feeding. The theory behind it is the more feedings your baby receives during the day, the less he may need during the night.

Sample Schedule 1

This is an approximate 3-hour schedule, which means the baby eats about every 3 hours throughout the daytime and during the nighttime as needed.

- 7:00 am wake up for the day, eat, play
- 8:30 am nap
- 10:00 am wake, eat, play
- 11:30 am nap
- 1:00 pm wake, eat, play
- 2:30 pm nap
- 4:00 pm wake, eat, play
- 5:00-5:30 pm catnap
- 7:00 pm bath, bedtime routine, eat, down for the night
- 10:00-11:00 pm dreamfeed (if desired)
- 11:00 pm - 7:00 am night feeds as needed

Sample Schedule 2

This is a transitional 3.5-hour schedule to use during the 3-6 month age range if needed before moving to a 4-hour schedule. Sometimes you skip this transition altogether, and the baby moves straight from a 3-hour schedule to a 4-hour schedule.

- 7:00 am wake up for the day, eat, play
- 8:45 am nap
- 10:30 am wake, eat, play
- 12:15 pm nap
- 1:45 pm wake, eat, play
- 3:30 pm nap
- 5:00 pm wake, eat, play
- 7:00 pm bath, bedtime routine, eat, down for the night
- 10:00-11:00 pm dreamfeed (if desired)
- 11:00 pm - 7:00 am night feeds as needed

Sample Schedule 3

A 4-hour schedule is common during the 4-6 month age range. The 4-hour schedule is a huge milestone! After your baby reaches the 4-hour schedule, he will basically be on such a feeding schedule indefinitely. As adults, it is most common to eat about every 4 hours during the day. After your baby is taking solids, you may end up adding 1-2 snacks during the day, which is perfectly fine.

- 7:00 am wake up for the day, eat (+solids if started), play
- 9:00 am nap
- 11:00 am wake, eat (+solids if started), play
- 1:00 pm nap
- 3:00 pm wake, eat (+solids, if started), play
- 5:00-5:30 pm catnap
- 5:30 pm possibly solids during dinner with the family
- 7:00 pm bath, bedtime routine, eat, down for the night
- Dreamfeed: This is usually the age range when you drop the dreamfeed because it becomes more disruptive to sleep.
- 7:00 pm - 7:00 am night feeds as needed

Schedules and routines for babies 3 to 6 months old often involve about 3-4 naps per day with the last nap of the day being a shorter catnap. Most babies are happy and content for about 1.5 to 2 hours before needing another nap or rest.

5

7-9 Months Old

Your baby is fully engaged with the world now. He smiles, laughs, and enjoys babbling with you. Your baby is likely also on the move! During the 7-9 month age range, babies can roll to their tummy and back again, sit without your help, and support their weight with their legs well enough to bounce when you hold them.

You baby's schedule is elongating as he becomes more awake during the daytime and stretches time between feedings.

Sample Schedule 1

This is a 3.5-hour schedule for a baby who still needs 3 naps per day. Transitioning from 3 naps per day to only 2 naps per day is challenging with some babies. 3 naps is too many while 2 naps is far too little, and by the end of the day, the baby is just too tired to make it to bedtime. One way to work around this is to keep 3 naps for a bit longer and simply shorten the naps up a bit. Go ahead and wake the baby up from a nap, keeping naps around 1.5 hours to 1.75 hours long. Continue to shorten the naps as needed to keep the baby on a 3-nap schedule until he is ready to transition to only 2 naps per day.

- 8:00 am wake, eat (+solids), play
- 9:45 am nap
- 11:30 am wake, eat (+solids), play
- 1:15 pm nap
- 3:00 pm wake, eat, play
- 5:15 pm catnap
- 6:00 pm solids/dinner as a family
- 8:00 pm bedtime routine, then eat
8:30 pm bedtime

- 8:30 pm - 8:00 am night feeds if needed. Talk with your pediatrician about what age would be appropriate for night weaning.

Sample Schedule 2

This is a 4-hour schedule for the baby who needs 2 naps per day. Most babies who fall closer to the 6-month mark will need a good 2-hour nap twice per day in order to feel rested. As the baby inches closer to the 9-month mark and beyond, you may find that shorter naps (about 1.5 hours) are more than enough.

- 7:00 am wake up for the day, eat (+solids), play
- 9:00 am nap
- 11:00 am wake, eat (+solids), play
- 1:00 pm nap
- 3:00 pm wake, eat, play
- 5:00 pm dinner with family
- 7:00 pm bath, bedtime routine, eat, down for the night
- 7:00 pm - 7:00 am night feeds if needed. Talk with your pediatrician about what age would be appropriate for night weaning.

Sample Schedule 3

This is an alternative 4-hour schedule for the baby who needs 2 naps per day. Again, some parents find it helpful to keep the youngest child on a slightly later schedule and the older children on a slightly earlier schedule. This can help free up time in the morning to get the older kids going and free up time in the evening to settle the baby into sleep and establish the foundation for a good bedtime routine.

- 8:00 am wake, eat (+solids), play
- 10:00 am nap
- 11:45 am wake, eat (+solids), play
- 1:45 pm nap
- 3:30 pm wake, eat, play
- 6:00 pm solids/dinner with family
- 8:00 pm bedtime routine, then eat
- 8:30 pm bedtime

Note: When your baby is ready (usually during 6-9 months) go ahead and drop from 3 naps to 2 naps. Then you will basically stay on this schedule (outside of maybe shortening naps and increasing wake time when needed) until your child is ready to transition down to 1 nap (typically during the 14-18 month age range).

6

9-12 Months Old

Finding a good rhythm and routine during the 9-12 month age range is usually a sweet spot for most parents. The amount of sleep children this age need does not change much, and the number of naps typically stays at two per day. Your child is likely moving around quite a bit by now crawling or standing. This is helpful because gross motor movement can put their energy to good use.

This is also a great age for mealtime rhythms because most babies this age can feed themselves finger foods, grasping items between the thumb and forefinger. This can help free up mom's hands a bit around mealtime and allow the baby to gain some independence with food.

Most 9- to 12-month-old babies are capable of staying awake for about 2.5 hours to 3.5 hours. Each of these schedules are variations of different wake times and naptimes as these babies become more awake and sleep less.

Sample Schedule 1

This is a schedule with approximately 2.5 hours of awake time before baby would need to rest again. This schedule still has about 4 hours between meals for baby, but the naps get a bit shorter and the awake time gets longer.

If you haven't already, this is a great time to focus on creating a good mealtime routine with your baby (see Chapter 15 for more information) and to allow the baby to enjoy the same mealtimes as the rest of the family both during the day and in the evening.

- 8:30 am wake, eat, play
- 11:00 am nap
- 12:30 pm wake, eat, play
- 3:00 pm nap

- 4:30 pm wake, eat, play
- 6:00 pm solids with family at dinner
- 8:00 pm bedtime routine, eat
- 8:30 pm bedtime

Sample Schedule 2

This is a schedule with approximately 3 hours of awake time before baby would need to rest again. You will again notice that the naps become slightly shorter and the awake time slightly longer, and baby still is able to eat about every 4 hours. If you feel the baby needs a small snack, feel free to add it in whenever your baby is hungry.

- 7:00 am wake, eat, play
- 10:00 am nap
- 11:00 am wake, eat, play
- 2:00 pm nap
- 3:30 pm wake, eat, play
- 5:30 pm solids/dinner with family
- 6:30 pm bedtime routine, eat
- 7:00 pm bedtime

Sample Schedule 3

After you get close to this schedule and routine, this is approximately where you will stay in a holding pattern until your child is ready to drop the morning nap somewhere around 14-18 months of age. This is a schedule where baby can stay awake for about 3.5 hours before needing to rest again.

- 7:00 am wake, eat, play
- 10:30 am nap
- 12:00 pm wake, eat, play
- 3:00 pm nap
- 4:30 pm wake, eat, play
- 5:30 pm solids/dinner with family
- 7:00 pm bedtime routine, eat
- 7:30 pm bedtime

The 9-12 month age range is a great time for many families. As you settle into a rhythm, prepare yourself for a few transitions in the coming months ahead. Your baby will drop the morning nap and shift his sleep to two consolidated chunks of time—one afternoon nap and nighttime sleep. However, with that change comes greater flexibility with schedules, and life gets easier.

7

12-18 Months Old

Congratulations! Your baby is one year old now. Your baby is also likely getting close to needing only one nap per day. This is the most common age range to go from two naps per day down to one nap per day in the afternoon. During that time, parents often experience a grey area where one nap is too little and two naps are too many.

Sample Schedule 1

This is a schedule for a baby who is very close to needing only one nap per day. Limit naps to about 1.5 hours maximum to help your child feel tired enough for the afternoon nap. The morning nap may become shorter and shorter over time until your baby is ready to drop it altogether. One telltale sign that your child is very close to dropping the morning nap—the afternoon nap deteriorates, meaning your child struggles with falling asleep or staying asleep during the afternoon nap. Stick with two naps per day for as long as your child needs. If you find yourself struggling to keep two naps per day, go ahead and try one nap per day for a week and see what happens. You can always revert back to your previous schedule if your child isn't ready for the change.

- 7:00 am wake, eat, play
- 10:00 am nap
- 11:30 am wake, eat, play
- 2:30 pm nap
- 4:00 pm wake, snack, play
- 5:30 pm dinner with family
- 7:00 pm bedtime routine starts
- 7:30 pm eat, down for the night

Sample Schedule 2

This schedule is another variation for a child who is very close to dropping the morning nap but still requires two naps per day. Some parents opt to decrease nighttime sleep when naps cannot realistically get much shorter during the day. This is a great way to temporarily bide your time for a few weeks until your child is ready to make the big change to only one nap per day.

- 7:00 am wake, eat, play
- 10:30 am nap
- 12:00 pm wake, eat, play
- 3:00 pm nap
- 4:30 pm wake, snack, play
- 6:00 pm dinner with family
- 7:30 pm bedtime routine, snack
- 8:00 pm bedtime

Sample Schedule 3

This is the coveted one nap per day schedule that is most common for ages 14 months and above. Initially your pre-toddler may struggle a bit with the transition, but stick with it for at least a week if you are able. Try to inch your way to the sweet spot of afternoon naps, which ideally take place about 30-60 minutes after lunch time. The first few days, your pre-toddler may make it until only 11:30 am. Keep trying to work your way towards the goal of a 12:30 pm or 1:00 pm naptime.

You may find that your child takes a good long 3-hour afternoon nap each day. Or you may find that your child starts to extend out nighttime sleep and takes a shorter 2-hour nap in the afternoon. Either way is perfectly normal. Do what works best for your child and your family.

- 7:00 am wake up for the day, eat breakfast, play
- 9:30 am morning snack
- 11:30 am lunch
- 12:30-1:00 pm nap starts
- 3:00-4:00 pm nap ends
- 3:30 pm snack (or whenever nap ends)
- 5:30 pm dinner with family
- 7:00 pm bath, bedtime routine, sippy or bottle with milk, down for the night

As you prepare to enter into the full-blown toddler years, life gets easier in some ways and more challenging in others. One nice thing is that the rhythms and routines you've been incorporating into your child's life are well known to him by now. These routines and rhythms are likely second nature to you and your child, making it easier for duplication among parents and other caregivers. The best part? Kids start to follow these routines without much prompting or instruction. Hang on tight! The toddler years are about to begin.

8

18-24 Months Old

Hold on to your hats, mama, you've got a full blown toddler now! By 18 months, your toddler will likely be having only one nap per day. This means more freedom in the morning to run errands, play, or go on walks.

The key to consider with this age group is again consistent naptime and bedtime. Whereas they are old enough now to have seemingly endless energy, they are in great need of regular rest to help minimize the tantrums that are so prevalent during this season.

Sample Schedule 1

With this schedule, you'll notice active playtime immediately after breakfast, leading up until lunch. The purpose is to allow kids the opportunity to burn and release energy. Following lunch is a bit of quiet reading time to help kids settle before sleep.

- 8:30 am wake up, eat breakfast
- 9:00 am playtime
- 11:00 am lunch
- 11:30 am reading time
- 12:00 pm nap
- 3:00 pm wake, snack
- 3:30 pm play until dinner
- 6:00 pm dinner
- 7:00 pm bedtime routine
- 7:30 pm bedtime

Sample Schedule 2

- 7:00 am wake up, eat breakfast
- 8:30 am independent play in toddler room
- 9:30 am snack, playtime with mom or play groups
- 11:30 am lunch
- 12:30 pm nap
- 3:00 pm wake, snack

- 3:30 pm park time or play outside
- 5:30 pm dinner
- 7:00 pm bedtime routine
- 7:30 pm bedtime

Sample Schedule 3

This schedule is perfect for the toddler who is a bit of an early riser. One tip we love to share is to save screen time for a slot during the day that **is not** before a scheduled sleep time because it often amps children up and causes sleep disruptions. Offering screen time before meals or after sleep is a great option.

- 6:00 am wake up, make bed, get dressed
- 6:30 am eat breakfast
- 7:00 am activity time
- 8:00 am free play inside
- 9:00 am independent playtime in room
- 10:00 am snack
- 10:30 am chores, playtime, or running errands
- 11:30 am lunch
- 12:00 pm nap
- 2:00-2:30 pm wake, eat snack
- 3:00 pm bath
- 4:00 pm screen time or reading

- 5:00 pm dinner
- 5:30 pm bedtime routine
- 6:00 pm bedtime

An important activity to incorporate into your toddler's day is the concept of independent playtime. He can play in his room, living room, or even backyard. This enables him to play with toys he doesn't have to share, get much needed downtime from external stimuli, and learn to spend periods of time alone without being entertained. It is also a fabulous option for teaching children to play alone without using an electronic device.

9

2-3 Years Old

When your toddler turns two, the days are both more freeing and challenging. Challenging because he is pushing the envelope and discovering boundaries both within the home and without. While he is able to do more things on his own like get dressed and perhaps use the potty, he is also entering into an emotional age where he needs your guidance, love, and attention more than ever.

Sample Schedule 1
- 7:30 am wake up, read, and play
- 8:15 am breakfast
- 12:00 pm lunch
- 1:30 pm nap

- 3:00 pm wake
- 3:15 pm snack
- 5:45 pm dinner
- 7:15 pm get ready for bed
- 7:30 pm reading with mom or dad
- 8:00 pm bed

Bargaining at bedtime can begin in full force around this age. It's important to show a lot of love, affection, and attention both throughout the day and at bedtime, but avoid starting a habit of bartering or bribing your toddler when it's bedtime.

Bartering is essentially a developmental milestone. Children will begin attempting to prolong the whole "going to sleep" part of bedtime and will ask for various things. The key to giving your child adequate attention but not giving in to bartering is being firm, kind, and consistent.

When your child begins bartering, note what things he asks for and include those in your bedtime routine. Whether it's a glass of water, prayer, song, or cuddle, tell your child what he can expect at bedtime and follow through. Then, when asked for something else, remind your child that you've done the bedtime routine but would be happy to add that tomorrow.

For example, if your child asks for another book, let your child choose the book to put on their dresser, and the next day, read that book with him. This will help him see that bartering is ineffective, yet still give him some decision-making power.

Sample Schedule 2

- 7:45 am wake up, breakfast, get ready
- 8:30 am activity lesson
- 9:15 am park time
- 10:00 am playtime at home
- 12:00 pm lunch
- 1:30 pm naptime
- 4:30 pm wake, snack
- 6:00 pm dinner
- 7:30 pm bath
- 8:00 pm bedtime routine, books, prayers
- 8:30 pm bedtime

Kids soak up everything at this age. Numbers, colors, shapes, and beyond. Their vocabulary increases as does their interest in their environment. Activities can range from basic coloring, drawing, painting, and play dough activities to more technical activities like STEM (science, technology, engineering, and math) activities or more intricate crafts.

Sample Schedule 3

- 6:30 am wake up, make bed, get dressed
- 7:00 am breakfast and clean up kitchen with mom
- 7:30 am play
- 8:30 am chores
- 9:30 am outside play and snack
- 10:30 am independent play
- 11:30 am lunch and clean up
- 12:30 pm naptime
- 2:30 pm park, exercise, or outside time
- 4:00 pm screen time and cook dinner
- 5:30 pm dinner and family time
- 6:30 pm bedtime routine
- 7:00 pm bed

By the age of two, children can understand the concept of helping you do household chores and duties. This is a great age to make sure they learn to do a few basic things like fold laundry, dust, empty the dishwasher, and put their clothes in the laundry. By having a certain time of day to do chores, your toddler will become accustomed to this activity and more inclined to cooperate.

10
4-5 Years Old

By the time your child hits the age of four, he is much more independent. He can generally dress himself, help with more chores, get his own breakfast, and handle his own toilet needs. While this means you can create a looser schedule, it's also helpful to have a few key times throughout the day that remain consistent.

Sample Schedule 1

- 7:00 am wake up, make bed, eat breakfast
- 10:00 am independent play
- 12:00 pm lunch
- 1:00 pm rest time in room
- 3:00 pm snack and free play

- 5:30 pm dinner
- 6:30 pm bath, stories, bedtime routine
- 7:30 pm bed

Sample Schedule 2

- 6:00 am wake up, make bed, get dressed
- 6:30 am breakfast then chores
- 7:30 am free play
- 9:00 am screen time
- 10:00 am independent play and snack
- 12:30 pm lunch
- 1:30 pm rest time in room (nap if desired)
- 3:00 pm snack and free play
- 5:30 pm dinner
- 6:00 pm bath and bedtime routine
- 7:00 pm bed

Sample Schedule 3

- 6:00 am wake up, get dressed, eat breakfast
- 7:00 am go to school
- 3:30 pm return home, eat snack, do homework
- 4:30 pm do chores
- 5:30 pm eat dinner
- 6:30 pm bedtime routine
- 7:00 pm bed

Your child will crave more freedom as he gets older, and this is a great thing! It's a good idea to keep some daily activities at set intervals and offer as much freedom throughout the day as your child can handle. 4- and 5-year-olds don't need a daily nap, but they will still need downtime.

Rest time occurs when your child goes to his room (or another allocated space in the home) with some quiet activities like books or drawing, and he has downtime. Every few days a nap might occur, but this is a time to cut down the sensory overload.

Rest time will benefit both child and parent. In order to have a positive rest time experience, we recommend dimming the room (but not making it completely black), keeping a few quiet activities at hand, having a noise level rule (for example, no loud singing or talking), and even deciding that your child must remain on their bed.

Many parents find success with giving their child books, busy bags, or a simple activity like a coloring book, and allowing the child to remain on his bed to do these things. This is very conducive to a child sleeping after they read for a bit as well because he is on the bed. This would also work in a reading tent, on a couch, or in a comfy zone of the house. As long as the child is not surrounded by noise or other family members, the specifics of rest time can be flexible.

As always, a consistent bedtime is key, particularly on the nights when no nap has occurred.

Section Two: Tips and Tricks

11

Tips for Managing the Day With Multiple Children

It's fairly straightforward to rock a routine with one child. Add another child, and it is slightly more challenging. Add another one or two, and well, you've got yourself a challenge. Impossible? No way.

When you're trying to juggle multiple children, let these key points guide you in creating your routine:

- Keep similar schedules where possible. If your kids are close in age, don't scatter mealtimes or naptimes. Keep them consistent.
- Decide a consistent morning wake time for everyone.

- Have set snack times. With multiple children, snacking can become a 24/7 affair if they are able to snack at a time of their choosing.
- Stagger independent playtimes if you want one-on-one time with each child, or keep the independent playtimes consistent if you need consistent alone time.
- Have easy no-prep activities on hand for smaller children while older children get screen time. No matter your screen time philosophy, the cartoons appropriate for 5-year-olds are different than those appropriate for 2-year-olds.
- Learn to corral. When you need to focus on something with one child, feed a baby, or complete a task that takes longer than 15 minutes, have the other children do something contained. This could be an activity in their room or for a smaller child, in a playpen or crib.

Sample Schedule for 18-Month-Old and 32-Month-Old

- 7:30 am wake up, diaper change, breakfast
- 8:30 am craft or preschool activities, more structured play
- 9:30 am independent playtime

- 10:30 am snack, free play inside, and as much outside time as you can manage
- 12:00 pm eat lunch
- 1:00 pm nap
- 3:30 pm wake, small snack, some screen time and then free play
- 5:15 pm dinner time
- 6:00 pm bath time
- 6:30 pm wind down to bed including reading books, brushing teeth, snuggles, and hugs
- 7:15 pm bedtime

Sample Schedule for 20-Month-Old and 36-Month-Old

- 7:30 am wake up, make beds, get dressed
- 8:00 am eat breakfast, wash dishes
- 8:30 am free play for both
- 9:15 am structured activity for both
- 10:15 am outside time, free play
- 11:15 am independent playtime in separate rooms/areas
- 12:00 pm lunch
- 1:00 pm nap
- 3:30 pm wake up and eat snack
- 4:00 pm screen time, reading, free play

- 5:30 pm dinner
- 6:00 pm family time
- 6:30 pm bath and start bedtime routine
- 7:30 pm bedtime

Notice this schedule is basically identical for both children. That's because they are both down to one afternoon nap and have similar sleep needs. You can tweak times based on the sleep needs of your child, but after 18 months of age until around 3 years, the basic sleep needs remain the same.

Sample Schedule for 4-Month-Old and 20-Month-Old

- 7:00 am wake up, feed baby
- 7:30 am wake up toddler and eat breakfast
- 8:15 am baby goes down for nap, toddler free plays
- 8:45 am structured play with toddler, activity, books, play a game
- 9:30 am toddler goes in room for independent play
- 10:00 am baby wakes up, feed baby
- 10:30 am toddler comes out of room, has free play, eats snack

- 11:15 am baby goes down for nap
- 11:15 am toddler goes in backyard or does activity inside
- 12:00 pm toddler eats lunch
- 1:00 pm toddler goes down for nap, wake up and feed baby
- 2:15 pm baby goes down for nap
- 3:30 pm toddler wakes up, has snack
- 4:00 pm wake up baby and feed, go for walk or to park with toddler
- 5:00 pm start dinner, allow toddler to help or put in playpen or crib for play
- 5:15 pm baby takes catnap
- 5:30 pm eat dinner
- 6:00 pm baby wakes up, bathe baby and toddler
- 6:30 pm start bedtime routine
- 7:00 pm toddler in bed, feed baby
- 7:30 pm baby in bed

You'll notice there is a stretch there in the afternoon where both children are napping (hopefully) at the same time. If the routine allows, it's a good idea to put both children down for nap together so you can use that time for yourself or other household tasks that are difficult with multiple children in tow.

Here are some tips for getting your children to nap at the same time:

- Be consistent. As with eating and waking, our bodies will acclimate to our habits. By putting your children down for a nap at the same time (say, 1:00 pm) consistently, they will begin to be tired at this time on a daily basis.

- Choose a time wisely. If your children have only one nap a day, choose a time soon after lunch before overtiredness sets in, and put both children to nap then.

- Don't begin negotiating. If you know your children need a nap, then feel confident in your knowledge that they need sleep! Put them down even if they resist.

- Ask your children to remain in their crib or bed until you come get them. One reason small children wake early is because they rouse slightly, and they know they can get up and play! If they are required by you to remain in bed until you come, this is often enough to encourage them to sleep a little longer.

- Explain your expectations. By the time your children are 2 to 3 years old, they will understand what you expect of them. This step is particularly important if you are changing their routine to accommodate napping at the same time.

- If they currently take naps at different times, start transitioning their naptimes together slowly. If they used to nap at 3:00 pm and you want to move it to 1:00 pm, this may take several weeks. You could go from 3:00 to 2:30 to 2:00, and so on. Unless your children are very self-controlled and sleepy, room sharing during naptime can be tricky. Why not put one child in their room and another in your room? Feel free to get creative with napping locations.

Give it time!

12

Daily Rhythms for an Only Child Ages 1-4 Years Old

A daily rhythm is something parents can follow without thinking about the clock or an approximate schedule based on times of day. The rhythm is simply the general flow of the day, and it can offer just as many benefits to families who are more appreciative of a daily ebb and flow rather than a set schedule.

Sample Daily Rhythm for 1- to 2-Year-Old

- Wake up
- Eat breakfast
- Get dressed

- Structured playtime
- Possible nap, if not free play
- Independent play
- Outside play
- Lunch
- Nap
- Screen time
- Dinner
- Family time
- Bath
- Bedtime routine

Sample Daily Rhythm for 3-Year-Old

- Wake up
- Get dressed
- Eat breakfast
- Do chores (put clothes away, empty dishwasher, and so on)
- Structured play (craft or activity, flash cards)
- Play outside or go for a walk
- Independent play in room
- Lunch
- Nap
- Free play
- Help in the kitchen

- Dinner
- Family time
- Bath
- Bedtime routine

Sample Daily Rhythm for 4-Year-Old

- Wake up
- Make bed
- Get dressed
- Eat breakfast
- Do chores
- Structured play (coloring, crafts, games)
- Free play
- Lunch
- Rest time
- Screen time
- Help in the kitchen
- Dinner
- Family time
- Bath
- Bedtime

13

Daily Rhythms for Multiple Small Children Ages 0-5

Routine has many benefits, but you will appreciate them even more when you have multiple small children in the home. With a baby, toddler, and preschooler underfoot, it's increasingly difficult to get anything done without some basic daily routines in place.

Daily Routine for 8-Month-Old, 2-Year-Old, and 4-Year-Old

- 7:00 am wake up, feed/eat breakfast
- 8:00 am chores for older kids
- 9:00 am nap for baby

- 10:30 am independent play for 2- and 4-year-old, milk and solids for baby
- 12:00 pm lunch
- 1:00 pm nap for baby and 2-year-old, rest time for 4-year-old
- 3:00 pm baby has milk and solids
- 3:30 pm 2- and 4-year-old get up and have snack
- 5:30 pm dinner, milk and solids for baby
- 6:15 pm bath, reading, family time, bedtime routine
- 7:30 pm bed for 2- and 4-year-old, milk for baby and bed

Daily Routine for Baby, Toddler, and Preschooler

- Wake up and eat breakfast
- Free play
- Screen time for toddler and preschooler, mat time for baby
- Nap for baby
- Independent play for toddler and preschooler, milk and solids for baby
- Outside time for toddler and preschooler
- Nap for baby, lunch for toddler and preschooler
- Nap for toddler and preschooler

- Milk and solids for baby
- Toddler and preschooler get up and have snack
- Free play
- Dinner
- Bath and bedtime routine
- Bed

Daily Routine for Toddler and Preschooler

- Get up, tidy bed
- Eat breakfast
- Chores
- Free play
- Independent play
- Run errands
- Lunch
- Nap or rest time
- Snack
- Free play
- Dinner
- Bedtime routine
- Bed

It can be difficult to meet everyone's needs with so much demand. What a busy season of parenting!

When creating your own routine or schedule to best meet your children's needs, it's helpful to pencil the must-haves into the routine and work out from there.

14

Sample Bedtime, Mealtime, and Playtime Routines

Ready for your day to start running even smoother? A great step to take is to incorporate more routines throughout your children's day. Keeping similar routines before bedtime, mealtime, and playtime is the perfect way to help children learn exactly what to expect throughout the day, minimizing the need for nagging, yelling, and reminding.

As children learn what to expect and master routines themselves, they feel more confident and tend to follow along with the routine without much instruction.

Sample Bedtime Routines

Pre-bedtime routines can vary in length depending on the needs of your children. Some parents enjoy a 20-minute bedtime routine while some take a more relaxed approach and use a 45-minute routine. At the end of the day, do what works best for your family.

Sample 1

- Bath time or wash up face and hands
- Change into pajamas, apply lotion, massage
- Small bedtime snack for younger kids
- Read 1-2 stories with mom or dad
- Hugs, cuddles, and a few deep breaths
- Tucked into bed

Sample 2

- Small pre-bedtime snack, if needed
- Change into pajamas, wash face, brush teeth
- Quiet time activity with mom or dad
- Hugs, cuddles, and a few deep breaths
- Tucked into bed

Sample 3

This is a bedtime routine that works well if you have kids four and older who are very independent. It works especially well if you are struggling with children who frequently come out of their rooms for another potty, drink, cuddle, and so on.

- Small pre-bedtime snack, if needed
- Change into pajamas, wash face, brush teeth
- Child plays in bed alone with books or a quiet activity until ready for bed
- Child is allowed to come out of room *only once* to say goodnight to mom and dad
- Say goodnight and tuck into bed

Sample Mealtime Routines

Keeping mealtime routines short and sweet is more than enough to get the job done. As children get older, the mealtime routine may include serving the family by helping with meal preparation, setting the table, and cleaning up after meals.

Sample 1

This is your most basic mealtime routine, and it's perfect for both babies and pre-toddlers. Most pediatricians recommend that kids of all ages eat at the table with other family members because it helps avoid eating while walking around or eating in front of the television.

- Wash hands
- Sit nicely in chair
- Prayer
- Eat as a family and use manners
- Sit nicely in chair until excused

Special tip: Maintain realistic expectations for the length of time small children are expected to sit at the table. Consider times that are developmentally and age-appropriate. For example, young toddlers may sit nicely for a maximum of 10-15 minutes at the dinner table before needing to be excused.

Sample 2

This is a basic mealtime routine that is easy for toddlers and above to use and understand. Even from a young age, toddlers can help contribute to a successful mealtime by placing forks and spoons on the table before a meal or carrying plates to the sink after meals.

- Wash hands
- Set table
- Sit nicely
- Eat as a family and use manners
- Carry plate to sink after excused

Sample 3

This routine is ideal for older kids who can share in more mealtime responsibility.

- Wash hands
- Help with mixing ingredients for meal or another meal-prep job
- Set table
- Eat as a family and use manners
- Help clear table and clean up

Sample Playtime Routines

Independent play occurs when a child plays alone without any siblings – usually in an area of the house with a physical boundary. This may be the crib, playpen, or bedroom depending on their age.

Structured playtime is a period of time when your child will complete a certain activity. This needn't be anything complicated, but it is a time that a child completes an activity with an objective. This may be painting, coloring, flashcards, art activities, learning activities, or reading time with you. Depending on your child's age, structured playtime may be an individual activity but will most often occur with an adult.

Free play is a time when your child plays free with no agenda. He may go from room to room or go outside, or he may do anything of his choosing that is within usual guidelines.

Family time generally occurs in the evenings when every family member is home. This may be dinner, couch time after dinner, daily devotionals, walks, or anything in between. It's generally a time where everyone makes an effort to be together.

It's easy to get creative with playtime routines throughout the day. A basic way to start is to simply have some sort of structured playtime at the same time each day. This may mean one of the following:

- Your children play independently in separate rooms at the same time each morning.
- Your children play together at the same time each afternoon.
- You all enjoy family playtime each evening right after dinner.

Regardless of the playtime routines you incorporate into your daily life, structured playtime that is the same each day can help keep everyone accountable when it comes to making quality time for each other.

You will notice that sometimes, we encourage the use of a timer. This isn't meant to be stringent or rigid in nature. Sometimes the timer is very helpful for children to understand that structured playtime ends when the timer goes off rather than after only five minutes. The goal is to help everyone (especially during family time) to commit to playing together for a set amount of time.

The timer is completely optional, and if you find your family does perfectly well without a timer, then by all means skip it. It is often just as easy to keep an approximate mental timer yourself and let the kids know when it's time to move on to something else.

Sample 1

This is a simple routine you can use to help your child play independently each day. If you are just getting started, you may want to start with as short as 5-15 minutes and work your way up to an age-appropriate amount of time.

- Create a kid-safe play area (playpen or room)
- Help your child choose toys to play with
- Set the timer
- Allow child to play for a set amount of time independently
- Timer goes off
- Offer appreciation or praise for playing well

Sample 2

To encourage children to play well together during a structured activity, incorporate this simple routine into your day. The structured activity may even be as simple as having the kids choose several toys to play with together. Or if desired, it could be a game, craft, or activity they choose together or that you create for them.

- Create a game or structured activity for kids to focus on
- Encourage kids to problem solve and play well together
- Set the timer or simply set a mental 1-hour time limit
- Allow kids to work through the activity
- Playtime ends
- Offer appreciation or praise for playing well

Sample 3

This is a favorite routine of ours because it encourages us to commit to family time each and every day. It's all too easy to get caught up in electronic devices and forget that interacting and playing together as a family is so important.

- Turn all electronic devices off and put away
- Create a game or activity to do as a family
- Set the timer or set a mental time limit
- Work together and enjoy the time
- Family time ends

- Offer appreciation or praise for quality time together and everyone does something of their choosing

15

Tips for Keeping Kids Busy Throughout the Day

While children are naturally "busy," they can tend to roam from one activity to another and one part of the house to another, all the while leaving debris in their wake. Just like the saying goes, *"Idle hands are the devil's workshop,"* kids behave better and the day goes smoother when they are busy doing the right things.

This doesn't mean you need to micromanage their every move, but it is helpful to structure their day in a way that allows them to use their busyness for good instead of mischief. A little mischief never hurt anyone, but chaos all day will quickly wear on both parent and child.

The key to having things that keep kids busy is thinking ahead. While some children's activities require a lot of planning and preparation, many do not. By having some go-to activities on hand using everyday materials (paper, scissors, cans, rubber bands, and so on), you'll find it isn't so difficult to occupy the little ones.

How to Keep Your Kids Busy Throughout the Day

Here are a few ideas:

- Create "busy bags" in advance where you put things children can play with like buttons, pipe cleaners, popsicle sticks with velcro, or even paint swatches. Use them when you need your child to be distracted.
- Stock up on coloring books, play dough, LEGO, and other activities, tools, or toys that are great for keeping your child engaged. Don't use them all day every day, but keep them to bring out when needed.

- Give them chores.
- Plan the night before some basic activities for the next day. It's easier to be prepared beforehand than to rush to find something when you really need it.
- Start independent playtime early. Independent play is a great way for children to remain busy and entertain themselves while you get other things accomplished.
- Use television strategically – not as an all-day babysitter. If you want your children to watch the television when you turn it on, avoid keeping it on all day as background noise.
- Create stations. Have certain areas in your home for certain things. A reading nook, a small table for crafts, and so on. You can direct your children to these areas when they become restless.
- Keep naptimes. Part of what creates that relentless energy often visible in toddlers is overtiredness from lack of sleep. Well-rested kids are calmer – or at least as calm as toddlers can be.
- Let them help. If you need to get household tasks done, let your toddler tag along. While the task might take longer, you'll know where they are.

16

Resources and References

Websites

A Mother Far From Home by Rachel Norman – No-nonsense thoughts for loving and nurturing moms. From physical, mental, and emotional aspects of motherhood to household tips, I tell like it is and like I pray it will be.

The Military Wife and Mom by Lauren Tamm – Around here, I write about practical parenting, enjoying motherhood, and navigating the ups and downs of military life.

Books

You may also enjoy these resources:

For the Love of Sleep: Practical Baby Sleep Solutions for the Everyday Mama by Lauren Tamm

Lies That Make You Pay: A Mother's Guide to the Frugal and Simple Life by Rachel Norman

Can The Kids Come Too? By Rachel Norman

17

Conclusion

Before I became a mother, I often wondered why everyone was so uptight about bedtime and staying home and many other things I found lifeless and boring as a twenty-something single woman. I thought for sure after I became a mom, I wasn't going to let it stop me from international travel, late evenings with friends, and outings whenever we pleased.

I was determined to avoid being the parent who allowed kids to "bog them down."

Nope.

Not me.

As it turns out, life with kids isn't as simple as living a free and clear day-to-day life with no sense of direction. Inconsistent routines and sleep schedules seem to breed unhappiness in our child-filled home nowadays.

International jet-setting with children is not for the faint of heart. Believe me—I've done it.

Late-night parties are rarely worth the time as they only lead to over-tired meltdowns with our littles.

Of course, we do appreciate regular outings into the world, but it's often during a time that works well for our children and offers something for the whole family to enjoy.

For our family, routines, rhythms, and schedules are a no-brainer when it comes to simplifying life with kids and enjoying smoother days overall.

Using the simple schedules and rhythms described in this book is one of the best decisions our family every made. Together we are thriving, discovering clear purpose in the midst of chaos, and maintaining our sanity as we travel the ups and downs of our parenting journey.

Rachel and I are so glad you joined along with us and allowed us the opportunity to share with you!

—Lauren, The Military Wife and Mom

Section Three: Printables

Download your 20+ routine and rhythm printables at this URL:

http://www.themilitarywifeandmom.com/printables/

Password: ROUTINES20

Please note that the password is case sensitive.

51320752R00054

Made in the USA
Lexington, KY
19 April 2016